Science for Smart Kids

Electricity

And

Magnetism

Colleen Kessler

www.RaisingLifelongLearners.com

The author and publisher specifically disclaim any liability, loss or risk, personal or otherwise, which is incurred as a consequence (either directly or indirectly) of the use and application of any of the contents of this book.

Please use common sense at all times.

DEDICATION

To the amazingly talented and inspiring writers of the Solon
Children's Writers Group , especially Mary, Eric, Janie, and Kate.
Thank you for always encouraging me to try new things. I appreciate
you all more than you'll ever know.

CONTENTS

Dear Parents,

Since all learning environments are different, there is no one right way to use this book. I personally prefer the materials and resources that I buy to be flexible and offer easy adaptability. I created this project with my preferences in mind.

I have set this book up so that it can be read and used as an independent unit study by your motivated and interested learner. The content is written directly to the child. It can also be read for fun if your child is interested in learning more about electricity and magnetism. You could incorporate it directly into your science curriculum and use it to cover elementary physical science for a portion of the year.

When I use resources like this with my own kids, I let them read the information and do notebooking pages independently. They record all of their learning and experiments in a science journal. In fact, we keep a science journal that continues until the notebook is filled. Every time my kids do any kind of experiment they follow the scientific method and write down the question they're answering, their hypothesis, procedures, results, and conclusions.

I set up bookmarked sites on our computer where they can explore more about the topics and play related games. When it comes time for them to try out the activities and experiments, I sit with them, but allow them to be the guides.

When following their interests like this, I want them to have ownership of the activities, so I try to be a facilitator rather than a teacher.

Throughout any study I do with my kids – whether they initiate it or I do – I try to set up a discovery table filled with related materials for them to explore freely. Some of their best discoveries have come from these setups. I've included a suggested list of resources on the next page.

Above all, have fun with your kids. The best lesson you can give them is that learning is a joy and lifelong learning is the treasure they should aim for.

I hope you and your children enjoy this book.

Hey Smart Kids!

I'm so glad you chose this book out of all the others you could have.

I hope you'll have as much fun reading it and trying out the activities as I did creating it.

Remember – smart people don't know all the answers. Smart people have all the questions, and they're not afraid to search for the answers.

Be a smart person! Investigate your world and seek answers to the questions you have floating around in your head.

Do you have an idea for another book of activities and experiments I should write? Got a topic you'd like to learn more about? Email me at colleen@colleen-kessler.com and let me know.

Yours may be the topic of the next *for Smart Kids* book!

Have fun and love learning,

SETTING UP AN ELECTRICITY AND MAGNETISM DISCOVERY TABLE

I believe that kids learn best when they are free to explore and experiment with new topics and concepts.

Consider setting up a discovery table for each of the units you study.

Collect some materials related to your study and set them out for your kids to experiment with on their own. When you get to the experiments and activities in this book, your kids will be excited to learn more formally and be ready to use the supplies in the way they are intended – and you'll have super-engaged learners.

So what should you include on an **Electricity Discovery Table?** I suggest:

Wires	batteries	buzzers	notebooks
wire cutters	battery holder	cardboard	markers
scissors	bulbs	metal brads	switches
tape	bulb holders	aluminum foil	magnets
LED bulbs	magnet wands	magnetic chips	magnetic balls
compass	iron filings	magnetic objects	nonmagnetic objects

INTRODUCTION TO ELECTRICITY & MAGNETISM

We take electricity for granted – until a storm blows through and we lose it! But, who invented it? Where does it come from? How exactly does electricity work, anyway? Let's explore together!

Start your investigation of electricity by making a timeline of important developments and people.

I've included a list of some interesting milestones on the next few pages to get you started. You can use the timeline pages included in this book to record the milestones you're most interested in to create your timeline. Simply write the date and details of each major development on the lines and draw or glue a picture in the box.

You may also choose to develop your own creative idea to share what you learn. There are web addresses below to some resources, but feel free to add your own through an Internet search.

There are so many cool things in the history of each scientific discovery and the study of electricity and magnetism is no different. Find those things that interest you the most.

It's important to remember that nobody invented electricity. It's been around forever, and has taken many scientists many years to figure out. In fact, people are still learning new things about electricity today! Here are some important dates:

- In 600 B.C., Thales of Miletus, a Greek philosopher realized that amber became charged and attracted dust when it was rubbed with a piece of silk. This was static electricity.

- William Gilbert studied Thales's work and coined the term *electricity* in 1600, after the Greek word for amber, *elektron*. He realized that electricity and magnetism were related and experimented with magnetic poles and current electricity.

- In 1752, Benjamin Franklin proved that lightning is a form of electricity when he flew a kite in a storm. He had attached a metal wire to the tip of the kite and a metal key to the end of the string. The metal wire attracted the lightning and made loose threads on the kite stick out and a spark jumped from the key when he placed his fingers near it.

- Alessandro Volta created the first battery in the early 1800s. He sandwiched wet muslin between metal disks, creating a charge.

- Hans Christian Oersted realized that there was a connection between electricity and magnetism in 1820 while performing a classroom demonstration and a compass needle moved when it was close to an electric circuit.

- The 1800s were a time of booming discovery related to electricity and magnetism. Inventions and milestones include the electric motor {1831}, Law of Electrical Heating published {1841}, Edison Electric Light Co. founded {1878}, Edison demonstrates the incandescent bulb {1879}, and much more.

There is so much more to learn about electricity than the few milestones listed here. Have some fun and read biographies about some of these scientists and look around the Internet for more information of the history of electricity. Links and more can be found on the Electricity and Magnetism Resource page I have on my website: **www.raisinglifelonglearners.com/?p=4291**

Electricity Timeline

Electricity Timeline

Electricity Timeline

Electricity Timeline

Electricity Timeline

EXPLORING STATIC ELECTRICITY

Have you ever seen a small **spark** fly after you've walked across the carpet in your socked feet and touched the doorknob?

Have you felt the small {or not so small} jolt?

I remember snuggling under the blankets in the middle of winter when I was young, and marveling at the small sparks that made their way from my feet to my belly when my pajamas rubbed against the wool.

These sparks are caused by **static electricity**. Pajamas and blankets rub together and electrons jump from one fabric to the other. During thunderstorms, giant sparks of static electricity – **lightning** – jump from cloud to cloud.

The air moves and causes ice and water droplets to rub against each other in the clouds. The clouds become charged with static electricity.

Positively charged particles rise to the top of the clouds and the negatively charged particles fall to the bottom of the clouds.

The negatively charged particles are attracted to positively charged particles on the tops of other clouds and on the ground, and jump toward them, causing lightning.

Cool, huh?

Write about a time you experienced static electricity. What did it feel like? Were you surprised? Scared? What happened?

Be descriptive and specific.

_____

_____

_____

_____

_____

_____

_____

_____

_____

_____

_____

_____

MAKE YOUR OWN LIGHTNING

You'll need:

- a completely dark room or closet
- a balloon
- felt, wool, or flannel piece of cloth
- a piece of metal like a tray or doorway

Try it This Way:

1. Put the piece of metal on a table or stand near a doorknob.
2. Grab the balloon and fabric, then turn off the lights.
3. Stand next to the doorknob or metal piece, and rub the balloon quickly with the fabric.
4. Pass the balloon close to the doorknob or metal.
5. Watch closely – you should see a small spark of static electricity jump from the balloon to the metal.
6. You just made lightning!

What would happen if:
- you rubbed your feet along the carpet before touching the doorknob?
- 0instead of fabric, you rubbed the balloon against some plastic wrap?
- you touched the door instead of the doorknob?

Write your observations below:

_____
_____
_____
_____
_____
_____

MORE STATIC ELECTRICITY EXPLORATIONS

Isn't static electricity fun? I love exploring it, and while making lightning is really cool, there are some other simple explorations you can try, too.

Hair-Raising Fun

Grab a balloon and a piece of wool. Rub the balloon on the wool, then stand in front of a mirror and hold the balloon just above your head. Watch your hair stand up toward the balloon.

Jumping Paper

Tear a piece of paper into tiny bits and put them on the table. Run a comb through your hair several times and hold it over the paper. Watch the paper jump up to the comb.

Bending Water

Run a comb through your hair several times and hold it next to {but not touching} a running faucet. Watch the water bend to avoid the static electricity.

THE ELECTROSCOPE

William Gilbert invented the first **electroscope** in 1600, calling it a versorium. It had a metal needle that moved freely inside and turned towards charged objects when they came near.

Over the next two-hundred years, the electroscope went through many different changes, all with the same goal in mind – create the best instrument for detecting electrical charges in objects.

First, a hanging thread was added that was attracted to charged objects nearby. Then, tiny balls made out of **pith** {plant fiber} were added to the ends of the thread to make it easier to see when the thread moved toward charges.

They would become charged when they got close to an object, and since they now had the same charge as whatever they were near, they would repel.

How far apart they were after repelling indicated how strong the charge was.

In the late 1700s, the electroscope was fine-tuned further. Gold foil leaves were used because the gold was more sensitive than the pith or thread.

In the activity on the next page, you can use aluminum foil to replace the gold foil. You'll be able to use your electroscope to check for sources of static electricity around you.

MAKE AN ALUMINUM-LEAF ELECTROSCOPE

You'll need:

- a jar with a lid
- clay
- aluminum foil
- scissors
- metal paper clip
- a balloon
- a square of wool or flannel

Try it this way:

1. Straighten the paper clip out.

2. Poke a hole in the lid of the jar big enough for the paper clip to slide through.

3. Push the paper clip through the hole in the jar lid and bend the end that is on the underside of the jar into an 'L' shape.

4. Form your clay around the clip on the outside and inside of the jar lid to secure it and make sure it is sealed tight.

5. Take a piece of aluminum foil and roll it into a 1-inch ball and put it on the straight {outside} end of the paper clip.

6. Use the scissors to cut a strip of foil about 5 inches by 1/2 inch. Fold it in half and set it on the 'L' shaped end of the paper clip.

7. Put the lid on the jar and close it tightly, sealing the strip of aluminum foil inside the jar.

8. Rub the square of flannel or wool vigorously on the balloon and hold it near the foil ball. Look at the aluminum strip

inside the jar. The ends should move away from each other due to the static electricity on the balloon.

Look around the house. What else might have a charge?

Write a list of things to test with your electroscope, and make a prediction as to whether or not it holds static electricity. {A few examples have been filled in for you.} Then, test it with your electroscope and write down whether or not your hypothesis was correct.

Object	Hypothesis	Result
Computer Screen		
Refrigerator Door		
Lamp		

CURRENT ELECTRICITY

Static electricity, for those who haven't caught on, is electricity that builds up in something. The charges build up until they jump to something else, like the spark of lightning that jumps from cloud to cloud we talked about a few pages ago.

Current electricity, what you'll explore in the next activity, is moving electricity.

If you want something to work – your computer, a flashlight, your brother's remote control car – the electricity needs to move through a circuit. A circuit is the path the electricity flows.

I like to remember that it's like a CIRcle since CIRcuit starts the same way.

No matter how complicated a circuit is, all circuits work the same way. Electricity leaves the source of its power, travels the path, and goes back to the other side of the power source in an unbroken path.

So, for example, in a flashlight, the power leaves the negative end of the battery, travels through the wires to the bulb, then through more wires and back to the positive end of the battery.

Have you noticed that electrical plugs have two prongs? When you connect the plug to the electrical outlet, electricity flows in through one prong, down a wire to the object that needs power, and out through the other wire and the second prong.

MAKING A SIMPLE CIRCUIT

What's really cool about electricity and circuits is that you can make one at home without any special equipment. Ready to try?

You'll need:
- aluminum foil
- tape
- a D-cell battery
- a small light bulb {maybe from a flashlight}

Try it this way:
1. Cut two pieces of aluminum foil and fold them into strips.
2. Tape one to the positive end of the battery and the other to the negative end.
3. Touch one strip to the bulb, just under the glass.
4. Touch the other strip to the silver tip on the end of the bulb.
5. The bulb should light up because you have created an unbroken circuit with your "wires."

If you really want to have some fun, play with this for a bit. Think about what would happen if you added two {or more} batteries, or more wires. Explore and draw or write down your observations.

MAKE A SIMPLE SWITCH

You know that **a circuit is a circular path through which electricity flows unbroken.** Now, you're going to take that simple circuit and add a switch.

When you experiment with batteries, wires, and bulbs, you learn that a current of electricity needs a power source. Batteries provide a direct current {DC}, while electrical outlets provide alternating currents {AC}.

If the current of electricity running along the circuit is broken for any reason, items {like flashlights, lamps, computers, and televisions} will not work.

Switches allow us to break the circuit to stop the flow of electricity – and turn things off. While inexpensive switches are available online on Amazon or other retailers, basic switches can be made with simple materials at home, too.

You'll need:

- a switch {usually under $2} or small piece of wood/cardboard with two metal thumbtacks and a large metal paperclip
- three pieces of wire
- bulb and bulb holder
- D battery and battery holder

Try it this way:

1. Insert the battery and bulb into their holders.

2. Connect one wire between the bulb holder and one end of the battery holder.

3. Connect another wire to the other end of the battery.

4. If you are making your own switch, lay the paperclip on the cardboard or wood, push a thumbtack through it, securing it to the board, and push the other thumbtack into the board across from the first so that the paperclip can be rotated to touch both, creating a metal path for electricity to travel.

5. Wrap the other end of the wire on the battery holder to one side of your switch.

6. Connect the last wire between the switch and the bulb holder.

7. Light the bulb by closing the switch so the electricity can flow through an unbroken current. Turn the bulb off by lifting the switch.

Now, explore again. Add more batteries and bulbs, try the switch in different places, connect things differently. Have fun! Draw or write down your observations.

THE LIGHTBULB

The light bulb is the result of many years and the work of many different scientists.

Beginning in the early 1800s, inventors searched for ways to convert electricity into light. In 1801, Sir Humphry Davy passed an electrical current through platinum strips. While they glowed, the strips vaporized very quickly. He could only get the light to work for a few seconds at a time.

In 1809 he invented the arc lamp. It was very small. Inside were two charcoal rods attached to a battery. It glowed brightly.

In 1840, building upon Sir Humphry Davy's success, Warren de la Rue created a bulb that contained a platinum coil within a vacuum tube. This worked very well, but as platinum was expensive, few people could afford such a bulb.

Joseph Wilson Swan was determined to create both a long-lasting and inexpensive bulb. He was successful in 1878 when he used a carbon paper filament inside a vacuum. By 1880 he was selling his bulbs all over Europe.

So, why do we remember Thomas Edison as the inventor of the light bulb?

While Swan was working hard in Europe, Edison was working hard in the United States. His goal was to create a bulb that would shine brightly for long, extended periods of time. He was eventually successful at creating a bulb that could glow for 12,000 hours. The incandescent design with a filament enclosed in glass with a screw-in base is still in use today.

What else can you learn about the development of the light bulb? Search the Internet or your library for more information and write about it on the following page.

_____

_____

_____

_____

_____

_____

_____

_____

_____

_____

_____

_____

_____

_____

_____

_____

_____

_____

_____

_____

QUIZ YOURSELF

You can use a simple circuit to create a fun game for yourself. It should make quizzing your friends for your next test a lot more fun!

You'll Need:

- Bulb
- Socket
- Insulated wire
- Poster board
- Construction paper
- Brass brads
- D-cell battery
- Battery holder
- Glue stick

Try it this Way:

1. Write some questions and answers, each on a separate square of paper.
2. Glue the questions in one column on the poster board.
3. Glue the answers in a random order in another column on the poster board.
4. Attach a brad next to each question and answer by pushing it through the board.
5. Flip the poster board over.
6. Attach the fastener for each question with the fastener next to its answer. Use short pieces of wire to do this.
7. Make a circuit using a battery in a holder, a bulb in a socket and two additional pieces of wire.
8. Leave the ends of the wire free.
9. Ask a friend a study question.
10. With one free wire tip, touch the question.
11. With the other free wire tip, touch the answer your friend gives.
12. If your friend is correct, you will have completed a circuit when you touched the brads and the bulb will light. If your friend is incorrect, the bulb will not light.

CONDUCTORS AND INSULATORS

Have you ever wondered why wire is coated in rubber, thick plastic, or another material?

Some materials carry electricity better than others.

These are called conductors, and things through which electricity cannot travel {or travel through poorly} are called insulators.

Cut a piece of wire and strip the coating off the tip of it. The metal inside is a very good conductor of electricity and the coating is an insulator. It keeps the electricity flowing along the circuit within the wire.

When wires are connected to batteries and bulbs, the bulbs light because there is a good conductor making a path for that current.

Insulators act as a barrier to the flow of electricity. In this activity, you can test different materials around the house to see what are good insulators and what are good conductors.

You'll Need:
- Three pieces of wire
- D-cell battery
- Battery holder
- Bulb
- Bulb Holder
- Objects made of glass, plastic, rubber, metal, wood, etc. to test

Try it this Way:
1. Connect one end of a piece of wire to the negative end of the battery in the holder.

2. Connect the other end to the bulb holder.
3. Connect another piece of wire to the other side of the battery.
4. Connect the final piece of wire to the open side of the bulb holder.
5. Touch the two open ends of wire to one of the items you wish to test. Does the bulb light up? If it does, the item is a good conductor. If it doesn't, the item is an insulator.
6. Test each of your other objects in the same way.
7. Record your results on the chart.

Object	Prediction Insulator or Conductor	Results

LIGHT UP A BULB WITHOUT A BATTERY

Head into a dark room with a comb and a fluorescent light bulb. Comb your hair 30-40 times in the same direction. Take the comb and touch it to the metal end of the light bulb and watch it light up!

The friction from your hair and the comb rubbing against each other causes electrons to jump from over to the comb from your hair. The comb becomes negatively charged, and sends that charge into the bulb, lighting it up.

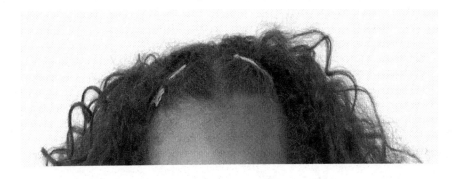

DIFFERENT TYPES OF CIRCUITS

You have built several simple circuits that contain one light bulb. What would happen if you added another bulb? If two bulbs were using the power from a single battery, the lights would be dim. A bulb is like a little bridge that electricity crosses on its way from and back to its power sources. The electrons slow down as they cross. Then they head back to the battery to recharge.

A second bulb will slow the electrons even further. They will have two bridges to cross now and twice the work to do. The bulbs dim. A third bulb will dim the lights even further. What do you think would happen if you added more batteries to the circuit? You'd have more power, so the bulbs would get brighter.

There are different ways you could hook up more than one bulb to your circuit. You could add another wire and keep the bulbs and batteries in a line. This is called a series circuit. Remember that electrons need a complete circuit to flow. If there is a break in a circuit the electrical flow will stop. The bulbs will go out.

There is another way to wire to a circuit so that all of the bulbs won't go out if one does. This type of circuit is called a parallel circuit. Each bulb is given its own little circuit to power it. The power from the battery is divided evenly between each of the circuits.

Draw a series circuit and tell what happened when you used your materials to make one.

_____

_____

_____

_____

_____

_____

_____

_____

_____

_____

_____

Draw a parallel circuit and tell what happened when you used your
materials to make one.

_____

_____

_____

_____

_____

_____

_____

_____

_____

_____

_____

_____

EXPLORING MAGNETS

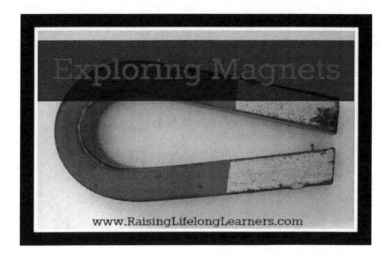

So far you've explored basic electricity -- static electricity, current electricity, switches, and a bit of history. Let's take a look at magnetism and how it is related to electricity.

Magnets are really cool to play with. Grab a bunch of different sized and shaped magnets, and play around with them, exploring magnetism in your home and yard.

Grab bar magnets, horseshoe magnets, wands, refrigerator magnets, and disks.

If you can order them {they're inexpensive, and really cool}, get some iron filings so you can see a visual representation of the magnetic field. These are available as loose filings and enclosed in plastic cases.

Check with your parents and see what you have around the house and order a few things you would like to try.

Along with the various magnets you've collected, grab different things to investigate for magnetic attraction. Try to have a large

Colleen Kessler

variety, including flatware, aluminum foil, buttons, ribbons, coins, small metal objects and toys. Put them in a pile and explore. Draw a picture of your explorations:

What have you discovered? Write about your explorations on this page. Did you sort your objects? How? What did the objects that were attracted to the magnet have in common? What else can you add?

_____
_____
_____
_____
_____
_____
_____
_____
_____
_____
_____
_____
_____
_____
_____

40

MAGNETISM

So you've had the chance to play with and freely explore some magnets and objects. Let's explore magnets a bit more.

Magnetism is the property of objects being attracted to other objects. All magnets have a north and a south pole. The area around a magnet is called the magnetic field. This is where the magnet's force is. The force of a magnet flows like electricity. It moves from the magnet's north pole to its south pole.

Magnets can attract each other. Only opposite ends of magnets attract. North ends are attracted to south ends, and south ends to north.

They can also push each other away. Like ends push against each other. For example, a north end of a magnet will push against another magnet's north end. A south end will repel another south end. This is just like how negative charges are attracted to positive electrical charges and like charges repel each other.

Some magnets can be very strong, while others are weak. In the next activity you can explore further. Find their magnetic fields using iron shavings. Test their strengths with paperclips. Try to make them attract each other and push against each other.

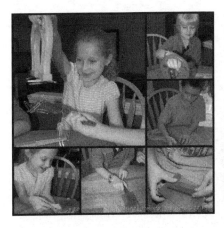

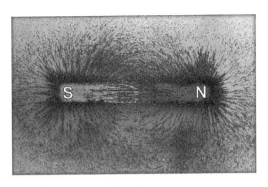

You'll Need:

- Iron filings (loose or sealed)
- Several different types and strengths of magnets
- Paperclips

Try it This Way:

1. Use the iron filings to identify the magnetic field for each of your magnets. Draw the different fields for different shaped magnets.

2. Take two bar magnets. Place them next to each other so that the north pole of one is next to the south pole of the other.

3. Push one towards the other. What happens?

4. Now, turn one of the magnets so that the south pole of each is pointed towards the other. What happens when you move one toward the other one?

5. How is this different when you use a horseshoe magnet? A circle magnet?

6. Spread the paperclips out on a table.

7. Look at your magnets. Which do you think will be the most powerful? (Able to pick up the most paperclips.) Which do you think will be the least powerful? (Able to pick up the fewest paperclips.)

8. Put them in order from the strongest to the weakest (in your opinion).

9. Test them by swirling each in the pile of paperclips, holding

them up, and then counting the paperclips that the magnet picked up.

Do this with each magnet and record you results.

Were you surprised? Why or why not? Does the size of the magnet make a difference in the number of paperclips it picks up?

_____

_____

_____

_____

_____

_____

_____

_____

_____

_____

_____

_____

_____

_____

_____

_____

EXPLORING ELECTROMAGNETS

In 1820, when he moved an electrical wire near a compass and the needle jumped, Hans Christian Oersted noted that an electrical current creates a magnetic field.

Michael Faraday discovered that the reverse was true a few years later – a magnetic field could also generate electricity. The relationship between electricity and magnetism was confirmed.

Electricity and magnetism have many differences though. A magnetic field always flows into itself and cannot be separated from its poles. An electrical current, though, can flow out and back into itself.

This is what makes it possible to use electricity to run toys, lamps, televisions, and other household items. Magnetism can pass through materials that electricity cannot like glass and plastic.

Electromagnets are made when an electrical current runs through a wire. The current creates a magnetic field that disappears when the electricity is turned off. Electromagnets can be incredibly strong.

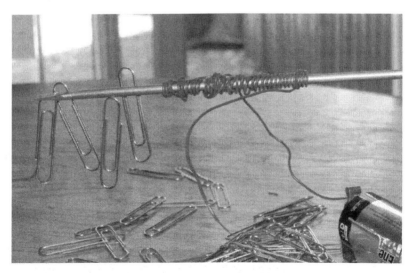

Are you ready to make your own electromagnet?

You'll Need:

- A long nail or screwdriver
- Coated wire
- Paper clips
- Battery
- Battery Holder

Try it This Way:

1. Wind the wire about 15-20 times around the nail or screwdriver.

2. Spread the paperclips on the table.

3. Place the battery in the holder.

4. Attach one end of the wire to the positive end of the battery.

5. Attach the other end of the wire to the negative end of the battery.

6. Drag your electromagnet through the paperclip pile.

7. How many paperclips did your electromagnet pick up?

8. Can you figure out a way to increase the magnetism so you can pick up more paperclips? Try adding another battery or wrapping the wire more or fewer times around the nail.

9. Draw your electromagnet and write about your exploration on the next page.

Electromagnet Explorations:

_____
_____
_____
_____
_____
_____
_____
_____
_____
_____
_____
_____
_____
_____
_____
_____

WHERE DO YOU FIND MAGNETS

Magnets are everywhere. They are used to make compasses. Doors have magnets installed to keep them closed. Astronauts use magnets to attach small objects to the walls of the spacecraft so they don't bob all around the inside.

Where else can you find magnets in your home? Go on a magnet hunt and write down all of the places you find magnets in your home and surrounding areas below:

Did you know that magnets also allow electric motors to work?

Magnets create pushing and pulling forces. Like ends of two magnets push against each other and repel. Opposite ends of two magnets pull together and attract. This pushing and pulling is what makes a motor spin. This is called rotational motion.

Next, try to build your own motor.

BUILD A MOTOR

You'll Need:

- D-Cell Battery
- Battery Holder
- Ceramic Magnet
- Enamel Coated Wire
- Wire Strippers (for adult use)
- Bare Wire
- Duct tape
- Pencil

Try it This Way:

1. Wind the enamel coated wire around the pencil in 30 tight coils. Leave several inches of extra wire free at each end.
2. Pull the wire coil free, holding it carefully so it doesn't come free.
3. Wrap the free ends of the wire a few times are the coil on either side. Make sure you wrap them opposite of each other.
4. Press the coil on a table so it is flat, even, and the free ends of the wire lay straight across from each other.
5. Have an adult strip the ceramic coating from the free ends of the wire.
6. Use two pieces of bare wire to make holders for the coil.
7. Bend each piece around the pencil to make a loop.
8. Attach the holders to the holes in the battery holder and secure with duct tape.
9. Insert the free ends of the coil into the loops.
10. Put the battery into its holder, blocking one of the connections with a small piece of paper. This will block the current until you are ready to start your motor.
11. Place the ceramic magnet on the top of the battery holder just underneath the coil.
12. Pull the paper out and give your coil a spin to get it started. It should continue to spin faster and faster.

MAGNETIC MINERALS

Believe it or not, many rocks and minerals have magnetic properties.

Have you ever visited the gift shop of a science or natural history museum and checked out the bins of inexpensive, polished minerals for sale by the bag? If you can, pick some of those up next time to test them for their magnetic properties.

Use this chart to record your findings.

Mineral	Hypothesis Magnetic/Nonmagnetic	Results	Discussion Strength of Attraction

MAGLEV TECHNOLOGY

The characteristic of magnetic poles makes some interesting things possible.

Artwork and reminders can be hung on refrigerators. Motors can be powered. And, objects can float.

Amazingly, when like poles repel each other, things can float in mid-air. They ride on the magnetic field. This is called magnetic levitation. It is known as maglev for short.

Maglev technology is being used in countries like Japan to power super high-speed trains. These trains can reach speeds of over 300 miles per hour. A maglev train hovers above a single track.

They move using the attraction and repelling forces of magnets. They can travel so fast because there is no friction to slow them down.

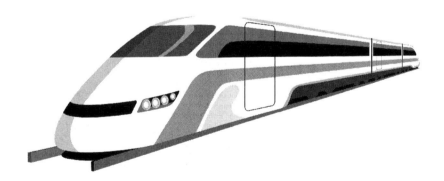

Use your own magnets to see if you can build a small maglev train of your own. You may need to experiment with the placement of your magnets.

The balance of magnetic force needs to be perfect to hold the train steady in mid-air. Have fun!

You'll Need:

- 24 small square magnets
- Double sided tape
- Poster board
- small foam board
- Sheet of plastic cut in half lengthwise
- Modeling clay

Try it This Way:

1. Place two strips of tape on the poster board in parallel lines about an inch apart.
2. Arrange 10 magnets on each strip of tape, equally spread out. Make sure the same poles of all magnets are pointed upwards.
3. This will be your "track."
4. To keep the train on its "track," use the plastic pieces to create walls. Stick the plastic to the poster board with modeling clay to hold it upright. Your track will resemble an open-topped box.
5. Cut a small rectangle of foam board so that it fits exactly inside the guide walls.
6. Attach a magnet to each corner of the rectangle, making sure that the pole opposite of the "track" is facing down so that the train is repelled.
7. Place your "train" gently above the track and let go so that it floats.
8. Give your train a gentle push and watch it move towards the other end.

Building a mag lev train is challenging. Tell about your experiences. What would you do to improve this activity?

_____

_____

_____

_____

_____

_____

_____

_____

CONCLUSION

In this book you've learned a bit about the history of electricity and magnetism, and have had a chance to play around with some cool materials.

But, this is just the beginning. There are so many more things to discover about the science of electricity and the attraction of magnetism for a smart kid like you.

I couldn't possibly include all there is to know.

That's why it's so important to be a lifelong learner. Smart people aren't afraid to admit when they don't know something. When you're unsure of an answer, or you're interested in a topic, take the time to follow your interests and learn more.

If you loved what you learned in this book, I hope you go on to study more about electricity and magnetism.

ABOUT THE AUTHOR

Colleen prayed for nice, obedient children of slightly above-average intelligence, swore she'd never leave classroom teaching, and definitely wouldn't homeschool. Since God has a sense of humor, she finds herself working from home while homeschooling her four highly gifted children who struggle with ADHD, sensory processing issues, and {you guessed it} obedience.

Life is never dull…

She has a passion for hands-on learning, gifted education, science and nature, and writing. She indulges these passions by writing books for kids, teachers, and parents from her teeny-tiny house in Northeast Ohio. Squeezing six humans, three turtles, and a dog inside a 790 square-foot house while working from home and homeschooling causes lots of chaos and challenges. But it also brings loads of opportunities to learn from each other and about the world.

Colleen blogs about parenting and homeschooling gifted and twice-exceptional kids, hands-on learning, and living intentionally at **RaisingLifelongLearners.com**.

You can join in the conversation, subscribe to the email list for a chance to win fun prizes each month, and to find out about new books as soon as they come out.

Made in the USA
Lexington, KY
10 October 2016